Around Maidenhead

IN OLD PHOTOGRAPHS

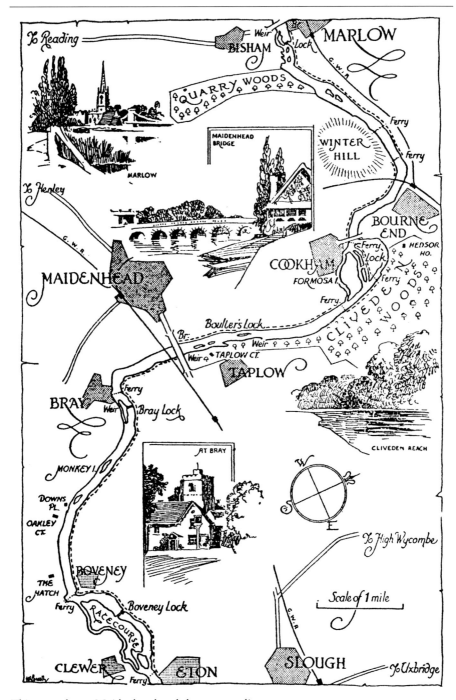

This map shows Maidenhead and the surrounding area.

Around Maidenhead

IN OLD PHOTOGRAPHS

MYRA HAYLES *and*
BERYL HEDGES

Alan Sutton Publishing Limited
Phoenix Mill · Far Thrupp · Stroud
Gloucestershire

First Published 1994
in association with Berkshire Books

BERKSHIRE BOOKS
Publishing imprint of Berkshire County
Council
Managed by Alan Sutton Publishing Limited

Copyright © Myra Hayles, Beryl Hedges, 1994

British Library Cataloguing in Publication Data.
A catalogue record for this book is available from
the British Library.

ISBN 0-7509-0712-6

Typeset in 9/10 Sabon.
Typesetting and origination by
Alan Sutton Publishing Limited.
Printed in Great Britain by
The Guernsey Press Company Limited,
Guernsey, Channel Islands.

This book is dedicated to David Hedges
who inspired and shared our love of the
Thames Valley.

Contents

Cookham Lock, *c*. 1885.

Introduction

This book not only extends the area, but also includes photographs not previously published in *Maidenhead in Old Photographs*. If it generates as much interest and feeling of nostalgia as that book, our efforts in the compilation will have been well rewarded.

The Thames forms a natural boundary and we have explored an area radiating about five miles from the town. Each place has its own identity yet all are closely linked with Maidenhead. The town was formerly shared by the parishes of Cookham and Bray, and it was not until 1451 that it came into being as a corporate body. Before this the site had many different names, with variations in spelling.

Throughout the ages the area has owed its importance to transport. The river was the first highway, and it was because of the construction of a bridge diverting the main road to the west from Cookham that the town gained in importance. William Camden, in *Britannia* (1586), stated that 'after they had built a wooden bridge upon piles Maidenhead began to have inns and to be so frequented as to outvie its neighbouring mother Bray, a much ancient place'. The main street was indeed lined with inns and posting-houses. Later the coming of the railway played an enormous part in its growth and prosperity. To the north, suburbs grew rapidly and the population quadrupled in the reign of Queen Victoria. Brunel's bridge, noteworthy for having two of the widest spans ever constructed in brick, also became one of the best known in the country when Turner painted *Rain, Steam and Speed*. In the 1920s and '30s the motor car brought in the socializing crowds and the river became packed with pleasure-craft.

On the south boundary lies Bray, which was once a royal manor and a Hundred. Its church and almshouses are of special interest and the village has many other notable buildings. Holyport, Oakley Green, Fifield and Ockwells Park all evoke the village atmosphere with their leafy lanes. White Waltham is dominated by the airfield, while Shottesbrook, Waltham St Lawrence and Littlewick Green also contribute to making this part of the countryside a pleasure to explore.

The old highway, the Bath Road, ran through Maidenhead Thicket which at one time was five miles wide. The thicket formed a barrier to the west of the town and had an evil reputation with travellers, who preferred to stay in the town overnight rather than attempt to pass through it in the dark. Burchetts Green is dominated by Hall Place with its wonderful surrounds. This was the home of the Clayton Easts but part of it was bought by Berkshire County Council and is now the Agricultural College. The route from Hurley to Bisham

The river and bridge were both very important to the formation of the town.

is a two-mile stretch of beautiful river and countryside leading to the grounds of Bisham Abbey. Bisham Church also stands by the river, and contains the historic tombs of the Hoby family.

Upstream from Maidenhead lies the manor of Cookham and some of its land is now owned by the National Trust. It includes Cockmarsh facing Bourne End, Cookham Dean Common, Cookham Rise and the Moor. Cookham, which once incorporated all of the town north of the Bath Road, is now a popular riverside village.

Many famous personalities have lived in the area and we have included some in the final chapter on popular events and celebrities. It is evident from this chapter in particular how the local residents have crafted the area around Maidenhead, and will continue to do so.

We hope this nostalgic trip is enjoyable. It is now up to us all to ensure that future generations will also be able to look back with happy memories.

SECTION ONE

Maidenhead – the Town

The High Street showing McIlroy's the draper at Nos 87 and 89. Their 'stocktaking sale [was] proceeding' – rather different from today's 'Sale now on!' Barclays Bank can be seen on the first floor with Mignon, a cake shop, next door.

An unusual view of King Street with the Bell Hotel on the left, 1939. Trains crossing the bridge would have seen the clock tower clearly. Cycling was very popular at the time, and there were several cycle shops in the town. These included Cox Bros, 63 Queen Street, Hildreth, 23 King Street, Timberlake's, 85 and 87 Queen Street, To and Fro Cycle Co., 2 Station Approach and Wilkins, 76 King Street.

High Street, Maidenhead.

As the main thoroughfare from London to the west, the Bath Road had an abundance of inns. Here The White Horse can be seen at the west end of the High Street. The road was open for traffic which eventually became so heavy that there were numerous traffic jams.

The guildhall on the right was built in 1777 when the market house was demolished. When the council took it over in 1836 it soon became too small, but it wasn't until 1960 that work began on the new town hall.

St Ives Hotel (left) in Ives Place was demolished in 1956. It was a sixteenth-century property which once belonged to Bisham Abbey until ownership passed in 1540 to Queen Anne of Cleves. The library stands on the right. Next to it was the war memorial designed by a former borough surveyor, Lt. Col. Percy Jones. When the present library was built, the memorial was moved across the road.

Upson's the optician, chemist and druggist of 35 and 37 High Street.

Brock Lane, thought to have been called Brook Lane at one point, had a National School which was eventually used as a Sunday School and meeting-place. It was here that the Cottage Hospital Fund was launched in 1877. There was also an Oddfellows Hall in the Lane.

The parish church of St Mary Magdalene, built by local builders Jones and Sons, replaced the previous churches which were situated in the centre of the High Street in 1270 and rebuilt in the same position in 1724. In 1842 the church was built at the east end of the High Street.

Edwards and Co., the tailors of 56 Queen Street, had an interesting shop front.

In coaching days Castle Hill was called Folly Hill, then the top was developed for housing by J. Clark. The building on the left, built in 1891, is often called 'the Folly' because of its appearance, or perhaps as a memory of bygone days. The drive up to the Terrace, with its elegant homes, can be seen on the right.

Maidenhead College was founded by A. Millar Inglis and built in 1891. It later became the Convent of the Nativity but reverted to its original name in 1978.

All Saint's Church at Boyn Hill plus the official seal of the corporation, often called 'the lozenge'. It was the seal of John Godayne, canon of Thiers. The picture below shows the dedication of the church, after extensions were built in 1907.

A view of All Saints' Avenue, from the church. It is still lined with trees but the postbox and the police box have gone.

The Queen Anne Hotel used to stand at the bottom of Castle Hill. The architect was Charles Cooper but the designer and manufacturer of the bricks and tiles is believed to be J. Hardwell of Pinkney Green Kilns who supplied examples of every kind of moulding that they made for the building.

County Girls' School, Maidenhead
The Lawn

On 24 January 1905 Maidenhead Girls' School (for a long time known as the County Girls' School) was opened at the Technical Institute with eleven pupils. The school moved in May 1907 to a house on Castle Hill previously owned by the Nicholson family, while Queen Anne House was also used.

County Girls' School, Maidenhead
A Class Room.

In 1959 the school moved to Farm Road and was officially opened by Princess Alexandra. It became Newlands Comprehensive in 1973. The headteachers have been: 1958–76, Miss Costello; 1976–90, Mrs Leighton; and since 1990, Mrs Brenton.

Maidenhead District Laundry Company Limited.

This Laundry has been inspected by His Majesty's Inspector and been found to be one of the best Sanitary Laundries in England—up-to-date in every respect.

Exterior and Interior views of the Maidenhead District Laundry, Furze Platt.

The laundry was opened in 1886 on the site of a poultry farm, and it provided employment for many of the local residents of Furze Platt. Here, a 1919 advertisement states: 'This laundry has been inspected by His Majesty's Inspector and been found to be one of the best sanitary laundries in England – up-to-date in every respect.'

The Golden Harp in Furze Platt still shows what its purpose was, besides providing liquid refreshment.

Crauford House was once the home of Mayor Pearce who was renowned for introducing electricity to Maidenhead. In 1890 he gave Kidwells Park to the town. At the time of this photograph, 1919, Crauford House was a school, and an advertisement declared that it 'imparts instruction on modern lines'.

Cordwalles School stood at the top of a hill, 1½ miles from the GWR station and was a high-class preparatory school for boys.

Spencer Farm gate, *c*. 1960, stood on land belonging to the medieval family of the Despencers. Aldebury Road and its surrounds has now taken its place.

In the earlier part of this century there was a boom in house building in this fashionable area owing to the proximity of the river. The Ray Lodge Estate was affected by the corporation when parts of it were bought to improve the entrance into Ray Park Avenue.

This picture shows the lovely Maidenhead Bridge and the Riviera Hotel with the rowing-club premises on the left bank. Judging by the number of spectators the event is probably a regatta.

Between the twelfth and eighteenth centuries there was a wharf on this site. The gardens were developed in 1945 after the Hungarian Club was pulled down.

The promenade became a meeting-place for people watching the boats at Boulters Lock. The road is named The Promenade in the top picture, and Raymead Road below, but it was also called Thames Road.

The Reitlinger Fine Art Museum exhibited local archaeological finds, prints, drawings, ceramics, carvings and paintings. It is hoped that the Heritage Centre will be able to continue to accommodate and display many of the area's 'treasures'.

The Guards Club, c. 1908. It attracted many of the socializing crowds. Its premises included the island in the centre of the river, and during the late nineteenth century Maidenhead became 'the most fashionable riverside resort'. Visitors included members of the royal family.

This scene by Edward John Nieman (1813–76) was painted in 1842. It shows Boulters Lock and Ray Mill House.

Raymead and Lock Island are up-river from Boulter's Lock. Many boats still moor here while waiting to go through the lock.

Though the Thames gave enjoyment and work, the menace of the river is shown here after flooding in 1894 and 1903. A flood relief scheme has now thankfully improved the situation.

SECTION TWO

Around Bray and Holyport

The Sounding Arch, Brunel's famous bridge, carries the GWR over the Thames. This view is from the Fisheries, an upmarket housing development.

In 1890 building began on the Fisheries opposite Orkney Cottage. Annie Smith's house was the first along Bray Reach. This 1908 postcard also sends a birthday greeting.

The original showboat in Oldfield Road was a popular nightclub. Oldfield was one of the common pastures of Bray parish – a place to practise archery at the butts and later to play cricket.

Monkey Island was made famous for fishing by Charles, 3rd Duke of Marlborough. The pavilion or banqueting hall is decorated with paintings on wall panels and ceilings representing waterside flowers and plants, and these surround hundreds of monkeys engaged in hunting, fishing and shooting. The gardens are reached by a bridge and the hunting-lodge, much extended, is now a popular hotel.

Braymead was built between 1901 and 1902 by F.I. Pitman. Bought in 1922 by a syndicate, it was then established as a hotel, and music and entertainment attracted many customers to its riverside terrace and ballroom.

HOTEL-DE-PARIS, BRAY, MAIDENHEAD

The same hotel, which by 1928 had been renamed the Hotel de Paris, Bray. It was so called after the Café de Paris in London, which shared the same owner. The hotel went into decline after the Second World War and was demolished in 1964, to be replaced by Braybank.

The landing place in Bray is a short way from Monkey Island and Bray Lock, and visitors arriving by river have a most favourable first impression of the village. The original Waterside Inn was once on the other side of the road.

The ferry at Bray, *c*. 1904. Ferry Lane has many protected buildings, some of them dating back to the fifteenth century. Ferry Cottage by the landing place was built in 1883.

Bray village in 1907 is a peaceful scene.

The lychgate of St Michael's Church, with its rooms above, has carved on it the date 1448 in arabic numerals. The church itself was founded in 1293. The card below, which has a postmark dated 1905, is titled 'Bray vicarage' but other buildings in the village have also been used for this purpose.

Bray, *c.* 1890. It was a charming riverside village with its half-timbered buildings. St Michael's Church rises above the houses. It was once a royal manor and Hundred but is probably better known for its turncoat vicar!

Ferry End, or 'Mustard Row' as it was known locally, is a row of cottages that looks much the same as when it was first built.

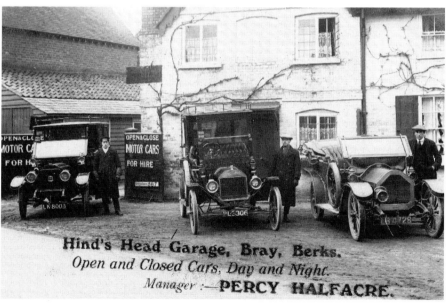

Hind's Head Garage, Bray, Berks.
Open and Closed Cars, Day and Night.
Manager :— PERCY HALFACRE.

The Hind's Head Garage was formerly used as stables for the fashionable hotel, the Hind's Head.

Braywick Road, 1890s, was very much a leafy lane, though it was much altered by the sports development after the Second World War. Below, the Hare and Hounds at Braywick advertised good stabling, and there are records of its existence before 1845.

Maidenhead aerodrome was opened in June 1929 but only survived a few months. These pictures show an exhibition, and the planes used were from Brooklands School of Flying. Alderman Cox, at the age of 92, took a flight.

Boys Class, Spanish Children's Home, Bray Court.

The Spanish Children's Home, Bray Court, *c.* 1938. This was a Victorian mansion that used to be on the Windsor Road. It was built for John Haig and then became a centre for social occasions. During the First World War it was turned into a hospital and then in 1928 became a school. It was later used by the government during the Second World War, and prior to its demolition it was owned by Archers the stationers.

Oakley Court was used by its neighbour, Hammer Productions, for film settings. It was erected in 1859 on ground known as Water Oakley Wharf and has now been developed as a prestige hotel. Its lawns sweep down to the river so it is fitting that this picture shows the armorial ensign of the Conservators of the River Thames.

Shoppenhangers Manor is not as old as it would appear because it only dates from 1915. However, as far back as 1288 manors have been recorded bearing this name. Charles Pascoe Grenfell purchased a manor in 1861.

This postcard shows Holyport Green, Plummer. Originally there were two ponds on the green, one providing water for firemen's pumps. The ponds were also used to soak wooden wheels so that they would swell.

The George was one of many inns at Holyport. Others included The Cricketers which closed in 1967, the Belgian Arms and The Queen.

Above, the houses to the right of the man and child remain nearly the same. The transport here is a horse and cart. In the later picture, below, seen from a different angle, the house next to the car (centre) had replaced the two houses seen above left. The post office house still stands.

Behind Holyport Lodge, which faces the green, stands the building which houses the Royal County of Berkshire Real Tennis Club. This can still be seen bearing the date 1889.

The Belgian Arms used to be called The Eagle but the name was changed when German prisoners of war, who were billeted at Philberds, began saluting the sign. The inn is thought to have been a hat maker's and until 1835 housed a Wesleyan chapel.

The Old Cottage and Elm Cottages on the right are good examples of eighteenth-century architecture and are still easily identified. The road leads down to the site of the picture below.

The Philberds in Holyport was a large house replacing the manor of Philibert, which in 1208 belonged to Roger de St Phylybert and which was destroyed by fire towards the end of the eighteenth century. The later building was so badly used during the First World War, when prisoners of war were held there, that it was pulled down in 1919. The remains of the wall and moat can still be seen a short way down from Hamble Cottage.

The Army School was founded in 1905 by E.G. Beckwith. It prepared boys for an army career and was run on public-school lines.

Ockwells Manor was built by Sir John Norreys between 1446 and 1466, using a timber frame with brick infilling. It has some famous armorial glass in its east window, and it is a fine example of a manor house of the period.

SECTION THREE

Around White Waltham and Littlewick Green

Greenwold is one of the attractive residences at Littlewick Green.

Highfield Bridge, *c*. 1891. The bridge carried the Great Western Railway, bringing people and prosperity to the area. Charles Batting's foundry, Maidenhead, built the bridges which replaced the original brick structures, while Isambard Kingdom Brunel was the engineer responsible for the construction of the railway. The Great Western Railway had been named in 1833 and the royal assent was given two years later.

Waltham Signal Box helped to ensure that the Great Western Railway ran effectively from Paddington. As early as 1824 it was decided that a link was needed between London and Bristol, and Maidenhead was once the first terminus westwards.

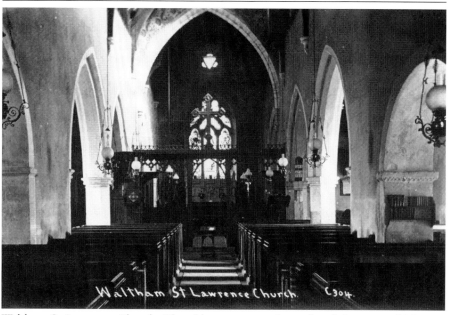

Waltham St Lawrence Church. The oldest parts are the walls of the nave which may date to the eleventh century.

White Waltham Church is situated on rising ground on the east side of a branch road running from the Bath Road. Bray Court Farm, the old manor house, stands opposite.

The fair at White Waltham is an annual event held in the grounds of Shottesbrooke.

The post office at White Waltham. Other names for the village have been Bury Town or Waltham Abbots.

This hanger was built by J.M. Jones and Sons of Maidenhead (1919–68). This was the first of many contracts for the Jones Company from the de Havilland Aircraft Company Ltd. in the 1930s for work at White Waltham, Harefield and Edgware.

Mr Ewers, featured in this group, was one of the local men who, together with others from British Airways and de Havillands, formed the engineering section. A ground crew consisted of nine men.

Tea-time at the airfield with Commander d'Erlanger, early 1940s. The aerodrome was built at the bottom of Cherry Garden Lane. Below, the Air Transport Auxiliary was controlled from the commodore's room and the operations block.

This historic building was the original site of the ATA until it became too small. There was also a mobile control van, distinctively painted in chequers. The picture below shows a Hudson which was used as a trainer.

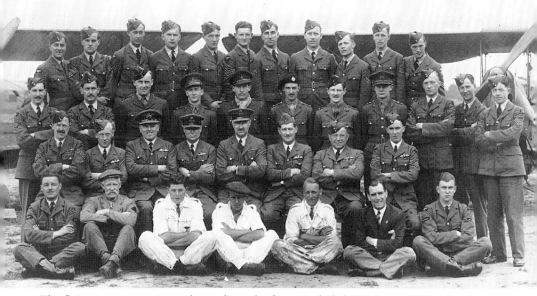

The flying instructors (second row from the front) included F.N. Scott, W.H. Maguire, H. Arnott, T.E. Wesson, B.P.A. Vallance, O.H. Lobley, A.C. Mills, W.M. Mackay, J.F. Schofield and T.D. Ainslie. In the front row, not in uniform, were the ground staff: Bill Hill, J. Ewers, M. Hutt, W. Evans and A.H. King.

An open-air service held at the airfield during the war.

Shottesbrook Church was built in 1337 by Sir William Tressel whose tomb lies in the north transept, and is situated in a manor that was owned by Alward the goldsmith in Rufus's time. Its magnificent spire is of the Decorated style of architecture and a rather unusual feature is that the nave is shorter than the chancel.

An aerial photograph of Woolley Hall, 1949. There are some noticeable features that no longer exist, such as the vegetable garden and hall chimney. The building on the bottom right became the Electricity Board's first canteen and rest-room, and an extension was built on the south-west corner at first-floor level.

Woolley Hall viewed from the south-west, 1880s.

The front gate and lodge of Woolley Hall, here shown in 1912, were replaced by William Cottingham in 1919. The gate opened on to the Bath Road.

Ivor Novello, born David Ivor Davies on 15 January 1893. The magic of his music, including 'The Dancing Years' and 'Kings Rhapsody', lives on. His home, Redroofs in Littlewick Green, was visited by many famous artists and it is said that 'We'll gather lilacs' was inspired by his love of the surrounding countryside. The house is now a stage school.

The annual Knowl Hill Steam Fair is one of the biggest of its kind in the south-east, although Appleford near Wallingford was the venue for the early steam rallies. This picture shows the impressive start to the chariot race. Enthusiasts travel many miles to

see these wonderful steam engines, and there are several other attractions, including veteran cars, farm machinery and animals. Craft skills are also demonstrated, and a good time is always had by all!

Here is a detail of a painting that was found in the stables of Woolley Hall. The picture was thought to be of a religious nature, but on cleaning it another picture was found painted underneath it. The original was by a fifteenth-century Italian artist. It was donated in 1963 to Littlewick Green and it now hangs in the Church of St John the Evangelist.

Sports Day at Littlewick, probably in the 1970s. The school, built in 1873, is still rather isolated despite its proximity to the busy A4.

SECTION FOUR

Around Burchetts Green, Hurley and Bisham

The Thicket at a tranquil stage in its history.

Now owned by the National Trust, Maidenhead Thicket once had a bad reputation as the haunt of highwaymen and robbers.

Burchetts Green took its name from the Saxon 'Byrechechurste', *hurste* meaning copse.

Burchetts Green. A small portion of this hamlet was in the parish of Hurley and the rest was in Bisham.

A group of students pictured outside Hall Place when it became an agricultural college in 1948. The building still had a portico which had been added to the front entrance of the mansion but it has since been removed.

The Norman gate was demolished in 1967. It was positioned where the drive turned south towards the village of Burchetts Green.

This unusual beehouse has ten sides and is one of the finest examples of its type in England. It was restored in 1979 and is a listed building, standing in the grounds of Hall Place.

The Drawing Room, otherwise called the William East Room, has scagliola work of entwined dolphins topped by cupids, which is meant to symbolize an alliance between England and Holland. William, Prince of Orange, and his wife Anne are portrayed in stucco on the other wall.

Temple House. The hamlet of Temple took its name from the Knights Templars, who were granted the manor of Bisham during King Stephen's reign.

The Norman church at Bisham, photographed at the beginning of this century. The church has a fine tower, and the Thames flows by its graveyard.

The dining room at Bisham Abbey with its wood panelling and tapestries was built by the Knights Templars, *c.* 1150. The abbey was the seat of Sir Edward Hoby, Speaker of the Parliament of Elizabeth I. The last of the Hoby family died in 1766 and G. Vansittart bought it in 1781.

In 1947 Miss Vansittart-Neale loaned the abbey to the Council of Physical Recreation in memory of her nephews, Berkley and Guy Paget, who had been killed in the Second World War. In May 1901 Sir Henry Vansittart-Neale had discovered a tunnel leading down to the river, and another interesting feature is the 'marker stone' which dates back to neolithic times.

Schoolchildren from Bisham School stand outside the church gate, *c.* 1910. The school is one of the smallest in Berkshire and in the spring of 1893 was recorded as having ninety-seven pupils. Mr Henry Atlee was the headmaster at that time. School records go back to 1879 but there are indications that it is much older.

Bisham village has some interesting, pre-nineteenth-century buildings.

The Bull Inn 'has extended hospitality for over 650 years to royalty, nobility and commoners alike'. In the distance, the road turns sharply to the left, leading to the church and school.

The Gatehouse and church, Hurley, which remains a peaceful and lovely village, largely unspoiled by modern changes. Its position was at one time guarded by a toll cottage, situated immediately opposite the entrance to the village.

Ye Olde Bell is a gabled and timbered inn dating back to 1135. It was the original guesthouse of the monastery and remains on the same site. It was also a stopping-place for coaches, until 1890. The barn has been converted to a conference centre.

These cottages at Hurley have now been demolished. The entrance to the church hall is positioned just past the buildings on the left.

Lord Lovelace's mansion, Lady Place, was the meeting-place for Whig peers, who planned to overthrow James II and crown William of Orange in his place. The mansion was built in 1550 on the ruins of the priory and was later demolished in 1838. A secret tunnel ran to the cellars of Ye Olde Bell.

St Mary the Virgin was the church of the monastery. During Elizabeth I's reign its clergy were paid extra 'danger' money when passing through Maidenhead Thicket.

Hurley Church was consecrated in 1086 by Osmund the Good, Bishop of Sarum. The Lovelace Memorial in the church is nearly four centuries old.

The Cloisters, also called the Paradise, surrounded the original quadrangle. Hurley Priory was founded by Geoffrey de Mandeville in 1086 as a Benedictine monastery.

Two large barns and a circular dovecot, built in 1306, were formerly part of the monastic buildings.

Above, the bridge over Hurley Lock; below, the lock itself, built *c*. 1790 and called New Lock. There had been a weir in this position made from wickerwork traps. Attractive backwaters exist because the river is divided by many small islands.

Pinkneys Green post office.

St James the Less at Stubbings was erected in 1850. This postcard has the words 'Pinkney Green', and indicates that the church was formerly in this ecclesiastical parish.

Pinkneys Green is largely National Trust property. The brickworks there provided most of the materials for house-building in Maidenhead and they are believed to have existed as far back as Roman times. The Girl Guide movement was founded in Pinkneys Green by Miss Baden-Powell.

SECTION FIVE

Around Cookham

Cookham High Street.

One of the commons of Cookham parish, pictured above, is Cockmarsh which is situated between Winter Hill and Cookham village. Together with Widbrook it was designated common land by 1272 and later a grant of commons was made to the inhabitants of Cookham by Elizabeth I. In the picture below, the organ-grinder stops for a chat on Cookham Moor. Note the monkey on the top of the organ!

Above (looking east) and below (looking west) are views of Cookham High Street. Bicycles were a favourite form of transport between the wars and some fortunate people owned a motor car!

This postcard is earlier than those on the previous page. It illustrates Cookham High Street without traffic, only a solitary bicycle! There appears to be no footpath on the right, so that front doors would have opened straight on to the street. However, very little else has changed over the years.

Bel and the Dragon can be seen in the above picture. Parts of this building date from 1417 and it is one of the oldest inns to hold a licence. The restaurant is now a very popular venue.

The Tarry Stone originally marked the extent of lands owned by the Abbey of Cirencester and before it was moved it was the centre for many village activities.

The organizers of the Cookham festivities in 1911 are, standing, left to right: A.E. Flood, Col. T.J. Atherton, E. Cooper, W. Spencer (father of painter, Stanley!), C. Shergold. Seated are Col. F.C. Ricardo and the Revd A.W. Batchelor.

F. Chalfont had a cycle- and motor-sales shop on the Pound. This picture, *c.* 1910, shows three forms of transport – car, motorcycle and bicycle.

Cookham Dean Church

Cookham Dean Church and School were built on land which had been part of Cookham Dean Common. The land was given by Mrs Vansittart of Bisham Abbey who was Lord of the Manor of Cookham, and thanks to the great endeavour of Revd George Hodson the church was partly built by public subscription. The foundation stone of the church was laid on 24 June 1844, and the building was consecrated on 15 May 1845 and dedicated to St John the Baptist. The Revd Hodson became the first vicar, and he stayed in Cookham Dean until 1869. The school was built about fifty years after the church.

CKD.5 THE WAR MEMORIAL AND CRICKET PITCH, COOKHAM DEAN

The forge in Cookham Dean Bottom was worked by Harry Hunt from 1880, and this picture, *c.* 1889, shows the site before the pond was filled in. The old well was also slabbed over like those at Lea Farm and at the foot of Well Hill. Hunt was succeeded by James Howard and then Harry Crockford.

Behind the house on the right was Carmonta Bakery, which was very much in the centre of Cookham Dean, with Curell's Garage opposite and the church nearby. W. T. Deadman was the baker there until 1952, followed by his son Kenneth, but the bakery closed in 1957.

Cookham Dean School was opposite the bakery seen in the previous picture, and can still be found behind the present garage building. The Usher twins, Agnes and Marian, and Nellie Bishop are the small group seen here, *c.* 1902.

Cookham Dean Platoon (Maidenhead) Battn. Home Guard, September 1941. K. Deadman is seventh from the right, back row.

As with all riverside villages and towns, the water has played an important part in the life of Cookham. It has brought both disaster and good fortune. Flooding in the past has covered the commons and moor, but the River Thames has also provided work in the wharf at Hedsor, as well as good fishing. In 1840 the wooden bridge proved to be unsafe as the timbers were rotting and it was replaced by an iron toll-bridge within thirty years. In this picture the Revd Scott is seen with his son by the ferry.

A pleasant Sunday afternoon can still be spent watching the decorated pleasure-boats and their passengers passing through Cookham Lock. There are many more craft on the river now.

This picture of the toll-gate is dated 1946. The toll-gate was on the Buckinghamshire side of the river and all traffic passing through paid the toll to the man who lived in the small house next to the bridge.

Cookham Lock was opened in 1830, following many accidents on the river as a result of navigational difficulties of the barges.

As well as working barges, there have always been canoes and punts for hire and nowadays motor boats, too.

The ferryman rows passengers across the river. It looks as though it was a brilliant summer's day when this photograph was taken as the men are in their shirt sleeves.

Islands were formed by streams flowing from the River Thames near Cookham Bridge. They are said to be named after the Danish Odin, as in 1896 a Danish stone battleaxe was found near the millwheel of the stream which divides the two islands we know as Odney. The Odney Club now occupies the area, but during the Second World War the American Army used Lullebrook Manor. Its officers occupied the large house, while Red Cross workers were billeted in the village.

Formosa is the largest island on the Thames. Sir Graham Young had his home there, built with timbers from a ship, but unfortunately it was destroyed by fire.

Quarry Woods provided a passageway from the 'miracle' spring near Bisham through Wool Lane to Cookham, via Grubwood Lane and Kings Coppice Farm.

The royal manor of Cookham covered the same area as the old parish which originally extended from Bisham to the river at Maidenhead Bridge, including Cookham Dean and Cookham Rise. In 1818 George Bangley bought the manor from the Crown and at this time many large estates were divided and new houses built. Much later Odney Estates Ltd bought the lordship of the manor and in 1934 the National Trust took over the commons.

This scene today has changed little from this picture, *c.* 1930. Although the road is wider, the houses still stand and the Gatehouse can be seen in the distance at the road junction.

This photograph likewise shows how little altered is the pretty village of Cookham. A stroll can still be enjoyed from the High Street, through the churchyard and along the riverbank.

Personalities and Events

Ivor Novello at a garden party, thought to have been held in Elendene, Cookham Road, during the 1950s.

The *Maidenhead Advertiser*, spanning six reigns, contains the history and development of the town in its records. This unusual 'personality gallery' was printed in the centenary edition of the paper, 1969. Some of the people identified by present personnel are: Louis Baylis, Norman Baylis, Tom Middleton, Mike Colton, Don Seal, Gerald Baylis, Dick Easton, Colin Bowerman, Phyllis Neale, Cheryl Lump, Tony Anderson, Ron Cordon, George Stewart, Derek Gale, Florrie Attfield, Kath Hight, Sidney Horsham, Jim Brown, Bruce Powell, Pat Hill, Dennis Hill, Robin Maguire, Frank Stevens, Eric Addis, Ron Holmes, Harry Carter, 'Buzzer Bee' (Derek), George Lawrence, Terry Haines, John King, Les Hemmingway, Stan Woods, Harry Coleman, Garry Craythorne, Cecil Norman and Trevor Woodward.

Wesley Walker, who wrote *The History of Maidenhead*, 1909. He was the forerunner of others who have continued to research and record local history.

Tom Middleton was the editor of the *Maidenhead Advertiser* for twenty-six years. His books on Maidenhead give a pictorial history that has been difficult to match.

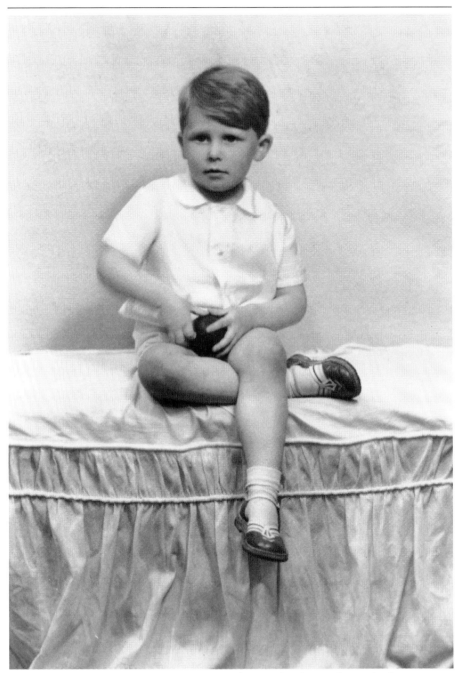

Who is this appealing young man? The clue is that he ranks with the previous gentlemen for his knowledge of the area. Everyone who is interested in local history should recognize the name – Luke Over.

Victorian Maidenhead can be seen
in the many photographs taken by
local photographers George Gude,
Norman Greville and others. These,
of the Bates family, are typical of
the records that have come to light
during the compilation of this book.

The 1891 Perambulation carried on the tradition of showing where the boundary of Maidenhead lay. Ancient stones and landmarks were checked and the boys beat them with flagged poles. Pictured below, 'Beating of the Bounds' in 1909 followed the same pattern. Mark Taylor is centre left in his town crier's uniform.

Lord Desborough inspects the 1st Battalion Berkshire Voluntary Defence Regiment, 1916. Many brave men from Maidenhead volunteered for this battalion, and some did not return from the Western Front.

Serving in the RAMC were members of the St John Ambulance Brigade from Maidenhead. Shown here are: (back row) W. Hare, W. Saunders, S. Hatch; (seated) A.W. Taylor, N. Moorcroft, T. Wetherall.

Lord Desborough hosted a reception for Maidenhead Corporation and neighbouring mayors, 30 July 1935. Those present included Alderman Cox, Councillor W. Thomas (Mayor), Alderman A. Upson, L.R.F. Oldershaw, W. Archer, E.B. Norris and H.H. Neve.

The Grenfell family, pictured in 1909. In the back row are Monica and Lord Desborough. In the front row, left to right, are Billy, Ivo, Lady Desborough, Julian and Imogen. Tragically, two sons died in the First World War and the third in a motoring accident. William Henry Grenfell inherited Taplow Court in 1867 at the age of eleven. He was actively involved in politics and sport, and was a generous benefactor, especially to Maidenhead. Pictured below, *c.* 1909, is the dining room where in later years his wife, Ettie, a renowned hostess, would entertain her guests.

Following the death of Queen Victoria in 1901 business was suspended throughout the country. Seen here is a gathering to celebrate the coronation of Edward VII. The *Maidenhead Advertiser* reported that the king adopted this title so that his real name, Albert, would be associated only with his father.

Maidenhead and District Sailors and Soldiers Recognition Day, 1919. A parade assembled at the moor, then marched through the town to Kidwells Park, accompanied by a military band. There, sports were played, followed by dinner at the cricket field. The day ended with a concert and a torchlight procession with fireworks.

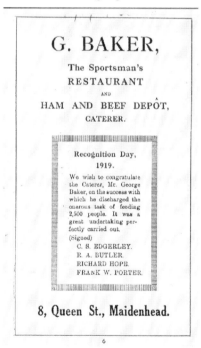

G. BAKER,

The Sportsman's
RESTAURANT
AND
HAM AND BEEF DEPÔT,
CATERER.

Recognition Day,
1919.

We wish to congratulate the Caterer, Mr. George Baker, on the success with which he discharged the onerous task of feeding 2,500 people. It was a great undertaking perfectly carried out.

(signed)

C. S. EDGERLEY.
R. A. BUTLER.
RICHARD HOPE.
FRANK W. PORTER.

8, Queen St., Maidenhead.

6

A High Street celebration for Queen Victoria's Diamond Jubilee, 1897. The Falcon Inn at No. 92 (centre left) has been replaced by Barclays Bank.

In this picture, from 1966, the Bowling Club committee and officers were: J. Carter, E.F. Halfacre, M. Huckins, F. Green, L.S. Moore, H.C. Distin, A.W. Bennett, S.G. Potter, A.J. Hooper, S.H. Lovegrove, G.M. Thatcher, L.E. Arter, W.F.C. Mead and R. Mortimer. Missing from the line-up are W.F. Reid, H. Davenport and J.A. Kemp.

Here the officers were Sir Ernest Gardiner, MP, Captain Henry Hoare, N. Naylor and Mr Barley. The annual subscription then was 12s 6d.

The Berkshire District Folk Dance Group at Bisham Abbey in the 1950s. Among the group are John and Adeline Finch, Molly Claydon, Sam and Enid Vickers.

Here, Paddy O'Neill is raised in the air as the finale to a country dance.

Playing the 'fiddle' for the dancers is Sam Vickers.

Here Sir Stanley Spencer works on one of his treasured paintings. He supported many local functions in Cookham, and below, he is receiving a Christmas decoration from Grace Johnson. It was at a Christmas bazaar that he drew a self-portrait.

Tables in Cookham High Street are laid out with Union Jacks to celebrate the Silver Jubilee, 1977. Surely the whole of the village must have turned out for this event!

The Silver Jubilee celebrations at Holyport and Bisham. The twin towns of Bad Godesburg, Frascati and Saint Cloud all joined in.

At Littlewick Green the 1977 Silver Jubilee celebration for Elizabeth II closely followed the Queen Victoria Diamond Jubilee programme. Below, the Revd. Bruce Hartnell looks at the poster for 1897.

A float from a hospital pageant in the 1930s. These 'Bisto Kids' were members of the Wednesday Club who met in Brock Lane. They include Eva and Peggy Fuller, Enid Bullock and Alice Turk.

Cookham Arts Club selection committee from the late 1940s included Henry Trivick, Victor Clark, Bay Robinson, Bert Felstead, Thelma Carstenton and Frank Sherwin. Showing the painting is Mr Philips.

Odney pottery club in the late 1940s. John Bev (centre) ran the John Lewis's evening classes. Also pictured are Les Knight (left), Ray Davis (front), Mr Spindler and George Body (right).

Celebrations at Moor Hall for Gaumont British, which made cartoon films. David Hand, seen here cutting the cake, was involved in the making of *Snow White*. Also present were Mr Stringer, Bert Felstead, Pat Griffin and Ralph Ayres.

The cast of the pantomime *Jack and the Beanstalk*, performed in 1953 in Pinder Hall, Cookham. Some well-known names include Jean Felstead, Moyra and Ann Hutchinson, Peter and Jean Gigg, Sara and Elizabeth Smyth, Celia Wetherall, Charles Elly, Mary Ash and Dierdre Blaney. The pantomime was produced by Bert Felstead and Christine Millard. The first pantomime was performed in 1951 by the art club and the next in 1952 by the British Legion. Pinder Hall has been the venue of many first-class shows, with casts made up of local people.

For over five hundred years the sovereign's swan-master with the Vintners and Dyers Companies have rowed the river marking the swans and cygnets which belong to them.

Braywood Memorial Hall in 1973 with Mr Raymond 'Teasy Weasy'. Several villagers acted as models in the show. Mrs Mary Snow is seen here sitting between 'Teasy Weasy' and his wife Rosalie.

The turf cutting ceremony for Cox Green Community Hall in February 1976. Margaret Brill (member of the Cox Green Youth Club), Revd. D.J. Cawte (Priest Missioner of the Church of the Good Shepherd), and Mr Clive Bullock (Chairman of the Community Association) have been identified in this picture.

Acknowledgements

Although many of the postcards and photographs reproduced in this book are from our own collections we must acknowledge with thanks the help from local friends and organizations in its compilation – especially the following: Maidenhead Reference Library, in particular P. Dobby, J. Fox, S. Gogna and R. Thomas; the *Maidenhead Advertiser* – David Ranger, the editor and May Powell, the librarian; Margaret Smith of Reading Public Library; the sales manager of Berkshire Library and Information Service, N. Bond; B. Brinkley; E. Burden; Angela Bolger of SGI UK, Taplow Court; John Davidson of Miscellania; T. Deadman of the Thames and District Cycling Club; Miss Dickinson, Lord of the Manor of Bisham; Heather Evans and Mr and Mrs Baines of Hall Place, Berkshire College of Agriculture; Mr and Mrs Ewers; Mrs Jean Hedger; Luke Over; Mrs P. Knight; Mrs E. Vickers; Diana Cook of Richard Way, bookseller of Henley.

We have made every effort to establish copyright and have obtained permission to reproduce when required, but if we have inadvertently omitted to do so for any photograph we offer our sincere apologies.

Lastly, for their patience and support, we thank our respective families.